Energy

by Don Herweck

Science Contributor
Sally Ride Science

Science Consultants
Michael E. Kopecky, Science Educator
Jane Weir, Physicist

Sally Ride Science™

Sally Ride Science™ is an innovative content company dedicated to fueling young people's interests in science.

Our publications and programs provide opportunities for students and teachers to explore the captivating world of science—from astrobiology to zoology.

We bring science to life and show young people that science is creative, collaborative, fascinating, and fun.

To learn more, visit www.SallyRideScience.com

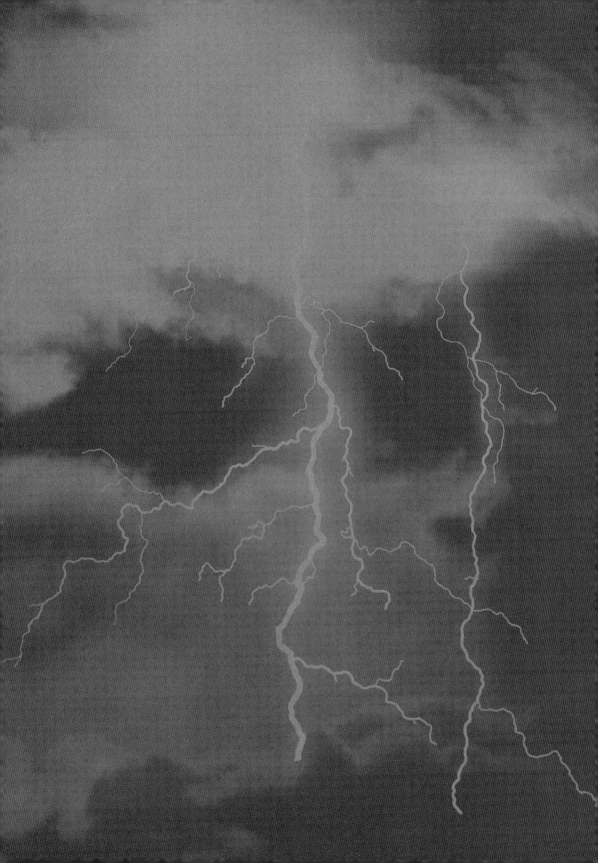

First hardcover edition published in 2009 by
Compass Point Books
151 Good Counsel Drive
P.O. Box 669
Mankato, MN 56002-0669

Editor: Mari Bolte
Designer: Heidi Thompson
Editorial Contributor: Sue Vander Hook

Art Director: LuAnn Ascheman-Adams
Creative Director: Joe Ewest
Editorial Director: Nick Healy
Managing Editor: Catherine Neitge

 This book was manufactured with paper containing at least 10 percent post-consumer waste.

Library of Congress Cataloging-in-Publication Data
Herweck, Don.
  Energy / by Don Herweck
     p. cm. — (Mission: Science)
  Includes index.
  ISBN 978-0-7565-3967-2 (library binding)
1. Power resources—Juvenile literature. I. Title.
  TJ163.23.H475 2009
  621.042—dc22   2008036546

Visit Compass Point Books on the Internet at *www.compasspointbooks.com*
or e-mail your request to *custserv@compasspointbooks.com*

Table of Contents

What Is Energy?

Did you just lift this book? You needed energy to do it. Did water flow from the faucet when you brushed your teeth this morning? Energy did that, too. Did you turn on a light today? Did you ride in a car, bus, or train? Are molecules flying around in the air? All these things happen because of energy. In fact, all day, every day, energy is on the move in you, around you, and throughout the universe.

What is energy? Energy has been defined as the ability to do work. That means that energy is the power behind making something move or happen. There are two types of energy: potential and kinetic. Potential energy is stored energy—it is not being used. Kinetic energy is energy in motion or at work.

Energy comes in a variety of forms. When you flip a switch and a light comes on, that's electrical energy. When the lawn mower cuts the grass, that's mechanical energy. Everything—including people—uses energy.

But even though energy is being used every second, it doesn't get used up. It cannot be destroyed, and it cannot be created. The total amount of energy in the universe doesn't change. It can be changed into various forms, but the total quantity of energy is always the same.

How Much Energy?

Scientists use a formula to show energy at work. They say that work (W) is the force exerted (F), multiplied by the distance (d). The formula is $W=Fd$. This makes sense. Pushing an object any distance takes energy. And it takes more energy to push a heavier object a greater distance.

Did You Know?

There are many forms of energy, including electrical, chemical, nuclear, thermal (heat), mechanical, and sound. All these energy types are forms of either kinetic or potential energy.

It takes more energy to knock a golf ball out of a sand trap than it does to hit it from the grass. The golfer must expend energy to move the sand as well as the ball.

Energy From Fire

People have long used energy to make their lives easier. One of the first energy "inventions" was fire, a chemical energy. The first known evidence of using fire for heat dates back at least 500,000 years—some experts say that it was even earlier. People used the energy from fire to cook food, heat their dwellings, and provide light.

Potential Energy

Potential energy is energy that is not being used. The energy is still there, but it is in storage, ready to be used in the future.

Chemical energy is an example of potential energy. It is stored in the bonds of atoms and molecules. Nuclear energy, which holds the nucleus together, is stored in the nucleus of an atom. Its energy is released when the nucleus is split or joined with another nucleus.

Potential energy from gravity, or gravitational energy, is caused by position. A ball resting at the top of a hill has potential gravitational energy. If the ball is pushed down the hill, its potential energy becomes gravitational, or kinetic, energy—it is being used. Water also has potential energy when it is trapped behind a dam. But if the water spills over the dam, its potential energy becomes gravitational energy, which pulls the water down.

The roller coaster uses kinetic energy as it climbs the first hill.

The roller coaster uses gravitational energy as it roars downhill.

Roller Coaster Energy

Kinetic energy is what gets roller coaster cars to the top of the first big hill. Gravitational energy is what causes them to go down. No matter how many loops, hills, or corkscrews come next, the roller coaster cars now have all the energy they need to complete the ride. There's only one catch. The upcoming hills and loops cannot be any higher than the first big hill. As long as something doesn't get in their way, the roller coaster cars can keep going up and down hills until brakes bring them to a stop.

9

Kinetic Energy

The second type of energy is kinetic energy—the energy of motion. Kinetic energy moves waves and creates currents in the ocean. Atoms, molecules, and all things in motion have kinetic energy.

Heat is a kind of kinetic energy that can be transferred between objects. It is called thermal energy. The movement of atoms and molecules in matter causes this energy. Sound energy, or sonic energy, is made when vibrating movement creates sound waves. Electrical energy is the movement of electrical charges. Electrons are tiny particles inside atoms. When they move, electrical energy— electricity—is released. Lightning is an example of electrical energy.

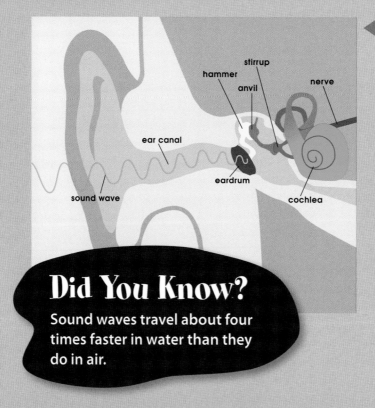

stirrup

hammer

anvil

nerve

ear canal

eardrum

sound wave

cochlea

Kinetic energy causes the eardrum to vibrate. These vibrations cause waves in fluid inside the inner ear. The waves are sensed by nerves, which send the signals to the brain, which figures out what kind of sounds are being heard.

Did You Know?

Sound waves travel about four times faster in water than they do in air.

Lightning and Thunder

Lightning strikes somewhere on Earth about 100 times every second. Lightning is a discharge of electricity in the atmosphere. This bolt of electrical energy can reach temperatures as high as 54,000 degrees Fahrenheit (30,000 degrees Celsius).

In just half a second, a lightning bolt can heat the air around it to a temperature five times hotter than the sun. The surrounding air expands from the heat and vibrates, making a sound we call thunder. Since sound travels more slowly than light, we hear the thunder after we see the lightning strike.

You can tell how far away lightning struck by how long it takes the sound of thunder to arrive. Count the seconds after you see a lightning bolt. Then divide by five to find the distance in miles that the lightning bolt is from you. Divide the seconds by three to find the kilometers.

Energy Sources and Fossil Fuels

Energy is everywhere and in everything. But how can we tap into all the energy resources in our world? What forms of energy are best for heat, light, motion, and more?

Fossil Fuels

In the top layer of Earth's crust is one of the most important sources of energy: fossil fuels. When plants and animals die, they decay in the soil. Over time, they are covered with sediment and pushed farther and farther down. Pressure and heat cause them to change chemically. With more heat and over a very long period of time, these remains become substances called hydrocarbons. They are now fossil fuels called oil, gas, and coal. Fossil fuels provide more than 60 percent of the world's electrical power. They make up more than 90 percent of the energy used every day.

To make electrical energy, oil and gas can be burned as they are. Coal, however, must be ground to a fine dust and then burned. The heat these fuels create is used to make steam. Then steam turns turbines, and turbines power generators to create electricity.

A coal mining operation

Fossil fuels also provide energy for travel. They make it easy for people to travel in cars, trucks, planes, and other vehicles.

Fossil fuels are an important source of energy that is used every day. But there is a problem. Fossil fuels cause pollution. Burning oil, gas, and coal can damage Earth and its atmosphere.

Fossil Fuels Everywhere

Everywhere around you are things made from fossil fuels. Gas for cars and even plastic bags at the grocery store are made from oil. Nearly everywhere you look are things made of plastic. Pens, toothbrushes, phones, cameras, televisions, computers, CDs, and more are made of plastic. All these things started as fossil fuels. Ink, paint, and crayons started out that way. And if you sleep on polyester sheets, the fibers in them were also made from fossil fuels. Without fossil fuels, many things around you just wouldn't exist.

Did You Know?

Fossil fuels started forming millions of years ago. Conditions need to be just right for fossil fuels to form. Most earth scientists believe that no more fossil fuels are being made.

Nuclear Energy

Nuclear energy is made by splitting the atoms of the element uranium. This is called fission. To get to this energy source, scientists at nuclear power plants shoot neutrons into uranium atoms. The atoms break apart, releasing energy and more neutrons. Those neutrons hit other atoms, which also break apart. This is called a chain reaction.

If left uncontrolled, the chain reaction will get out of control. At nuclear power plants, control rods are used to keep nuclear fission under control. The rods are made of chemical elements that naturally absorb some of the neutrons that are released. That way, there is not a huge chain reaction, which could be dangerous.

A nuclear power generating facility

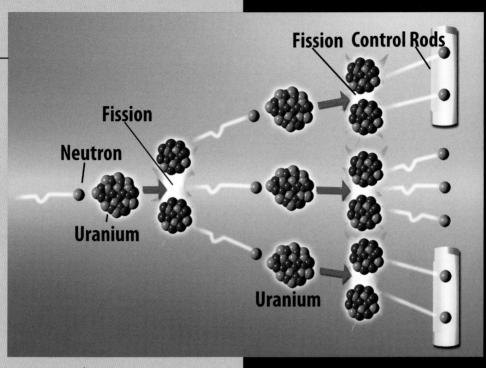

Nuclear chain reaction

Nuclear power makes about 11 percent of the world's energy. It makes a great deal of energy from a very small amount of fuel. Nuclear power costs about the same as coal power, but it generates less air pollution. However, nuclear pollution is radioactive and very dangerous. It takes special care and handling. The radioactive waste has to be sealed and buried for many years before the radioactivity will go away.

Don't Break the Chain

In 1942, a nuclear chain reaction was achieved for the first time. It made enough energy to light a small flashlight. That was a small but significant beginning. By 1945, three nuclear bombs had been developed and detonated. Two of the bombs—a test bomb in New Mexico and a bomb dropped on Nagasaki, Japan, during World War II—exploded by splitting the atoms of the element plutonium. The third bomb—dropped on Hiroshima, Japan—split the atoms of uranium. Today nuclear energy provides power for entire cities and more.

Solar Energy

Energy from the sun is called solar power. To use solar power, solar cells change light into electricity. The sun's heat can also be used to warm water for homes, businesses, or swimming pools. Water is pumped through pipes in glass panels called solar thermal collectors. Solar power works best where there is a lot of sunshine.

The best part about solar energy is that sunlight is free. But the solar panels are not. The cost of building solar power stations is very high. But once the stations are built, solar power is one of the cheapest energy sources available. It also creates no pollution, although the materials used to collect and store solar energy do create some waste.

Another drawback is that solar power doesn't work at night or when clouds block the sun's rays. Solar energy needs to be stored to use when the sun is not shining. For sunny areas, solar power is a good option for energy.

How to Help

You can make a difference in energy use. Start with your school. Schools in large cities waste up to 25 percent of their energy. You can help by talking with your teacher, counselor, or principal about an energy audit.

In an energy audit, students review the energy used. They do it by walking through the school and making notes. Look for lights left on when not needed. Look for windows and doors that are left open or not sealed. They let heat or air-conditioned air escape. Then look for appliances or lights that waste energy because they are old or in need of repair. A project like this could make a big difference at your school—and in the world.

Large fields of solar panels ➡ gather power that can then be distributed to nearby cities.

Wind Energy

Another source of energy is the wind. Actually, the real source of wind energy is the sun. Wind is a result of the way the sun unevenly heats the atmosphere. As warm air rises, other air blows in to take its place. The moving air is what we feel as wind.

For centuries, people have used windmills to use the energy of the wind. The propellerlike blades on these towers turn when the wind blows. The energy from this motion can be used to pump water, grind grain, or power a generator to make electricity. Most modern windmills are called wind turbines or wind generators.

Wind is free and has no waste. But you can't always guess where wind will be or what it will do. Wind energy is renewable, because wind keeps blowing. Wind power is the fastest-growing energy source in the world.

Modern windmills use propellers to create wind energy for our use.

Another energy made possible by the sun is wave energy. Ocean waves are caused by the gravitational pull of the sun and moon. One of the best ways to get energy from waves is to make a water chamber. In the chamber, the rising and falling of the waves causes air to be pushed through a shaft. A turbine in the shaft is used to make electricity. Wave energy is free and has no waste.

Did You Know?

The amount of power produced by waves varies depending on what part of the world you are in. The best places for wave power are the western coasts of Scotland, northern Canada, southern Africa, Australia, and the northwestern coast of the United States.

Scientists are hard at work developing ways to harness the power of the ocean, too.

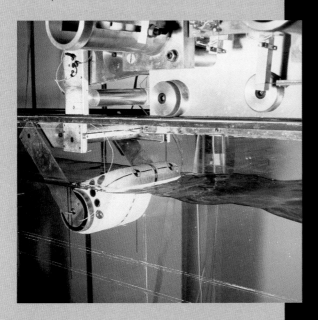

Wave Tank Experiment

Salter's Duck is a wave energy machine. It is being tested as a source for electricity from the waves of the ocean. A small model of the "duck" (left) shows how the large model works. The energy from the waves is absorbed by the curved body of the duck. It stops about 90 percent of the wave motions and then turns 90 percent of that into electricity. The device bobs up and down, rotating an axle. The rotating motion is converted into electricity.

19

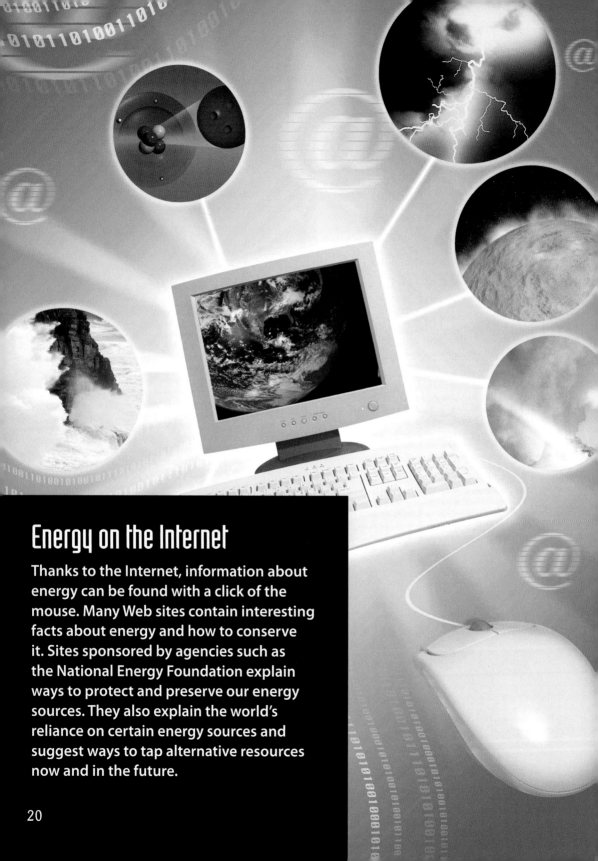

Energy on the Internet

Thanks to the Internet, information about energy can be found with a click of the mouse. Many Web sites contain interesting facts about energy and how to conserve it. Sites sponsored by agencies such as the National Energy Foundation explain ways to protect and preserve our energy sources. They also explain the world's reliance on certain energy sources and suggest ways to tap alternative resources now and in the future.

Hydroelectric power uses the potential energy of water trapped behind a dam. Water power stations generate about 20 percent of the world's electricity. The energy is changed into electricity by letting some of the water flow through tunnels in the dam. The water turns turbines in the tunnels, which makes electricity.

The generators are located inside the great curved wall of the Hoover Dam.

The good thing about hydroelectric energy is that it makes a lot of power cheaply. Fossil fuel is not required to run hydroelectric power plants, making them unaffected by increases in the costs of oil and gas. There is also no waste or pollution, and no dangerous hydrocarbons are emitted into the air. Operating costs are low since the plants are almost entirely automated. Water can pass through the tunnels in the dam all the time, continually providing the turbines with power to make electricity.

The drawback of hydroelectric energy is that water power stations are costly to build. And they can't be built just anywhere. There has to be a lot of water. And dams always change the environment downstream. The Glen Canyon Dam on the Colorado River in the Grand Canyon caused erosion from the ever-changing bursts of water coming out of the turbines.

21

Geothermal Energy

Deep inside Earth is a powerful energy source. It is called geothermal energy. The deeper you go toward the center of the planet, the hotter it gets. We know from mining and drilling near the surface of Earth that temperatures rise 1.1 F (2 C) for every 120 feet (36.6 meters). That means the center of Earth's core should be 180,000 F (100,000 C). But no one believes Earth is that hot. Scientists believe that the rate of increase must slow down, and the core is probably no hotter than 9,000 F (5,000 C).

But no matter how hot Earth's center is, there is a lot of energy stored inside our planet. Geothermal power can be mined in several ways. One way is by drilling wells into cracks in rocks where the groundwater is hot. The hot water or steam either flows up or is pumped up to turn turbines that make electricity. Another way to use this power is by pumping water down to hot rocks in the earth. The water turns to steam, which comes up through pipes and turns turbines. The turbines then drive electric generators.

Did You Know?

The word *geothermal* comes from the Greek words *geo* (earth) and *therme* (heat).

Geothermal energy is produced 4,000 miles (6,400 km) below Earth's surface.

Plant and animal waste, called biomass, can be used as fuel. This is called bioenergy or biofuel. People have been using this type of fuel ever since people began burning wood. Today wood is still the largest source of biomass energy. Biofuel also includes food crops, plants, industrial waste, and the alcohol made from sugarcane. Even the fumes from landfills—a natural gas called methane—are a source of bioenergy. Because this type of energy uses waste materials, it uses up less of Earth's resources than some other forms of energy.

To be considered a biofuel, the fuel must be made from at least 80 percent renewable materials. ▼

Corn-Fed

You would need only about half an acre (0.2 hectares) of corn to make enough fuel to drive your car across the country. Fuel made from corn and other plants such as sugarcane is called ethanol. It can be used as an alternative to gasoline. Using corn as a source for fuel can lower our reliance on fossil fuels. However, it has been argued that using food for fuel could cause food shortages and increased food prices.

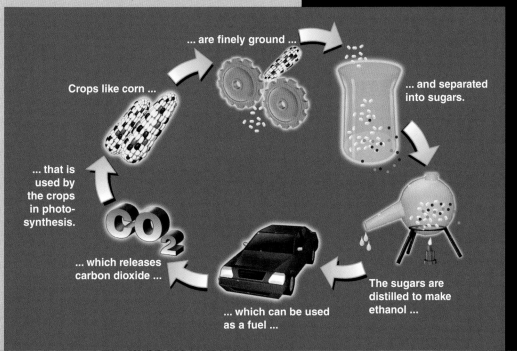

Crops like corn ...

... are finely ground ...

... and separated into sugars.

The sugars are distilled to make ethanol ...

... which can be used as a fuel ...

... which releases carbon dioxide ...

CO_2

... that is used by the crops in photosynthesis.

Using Energy

In Our Homes

About 22 percent of all energy used worldwide is used in homes. People use energy to heat and cool their homes. They use it to refrigerate their food and heat their water. The rest is used for lights and appliances like stoves, hair dryers, televisions, and computers. Gas, electricity, oil, and propane are some of the energy sources used to power our homes.

People can cut a great deal of waste by using the three R's: reduce, reuse, and recycle.

Did You Know?

Recycling one aluminum can saves enough energy to run a television for three hours. The amount of wood and paper thrown away each year is enough to heat 50,000 homes for 20 years.

At Work

Businesses use about 20 percent of all the energy used in the world. Office buildings, hotels, shopping malls, libraries, stores, places of worship, and warehouses all need power to function. Businesses have a variety of needs.

But in general, they use more than half of their energy for lighting and heating their buildings. The rest is used for heating water, air conditioning, cooking, refrigeration, and more.

Businesses use energy for lighting, heating, and communications.

Pumping Up

The average American uses 500 gallons (1,900 liters) of gasoline a year. But around 13 of these gallons (50 liters) go to waste because vehicle tires are not inflated enough. When you multiply this number with the number of cars, that comes out to billions of wasted gallons of gasoline each year.

In Manufacturing

Manufacturing has a huge array of energy needs. Industries use about 33 percent of all the energy used in the world. Some use a lot more energy than others. Oil refining uses the greatest amount of energy. Most of the energy used in manufacturing is used to make or change raw goods into finished goods.

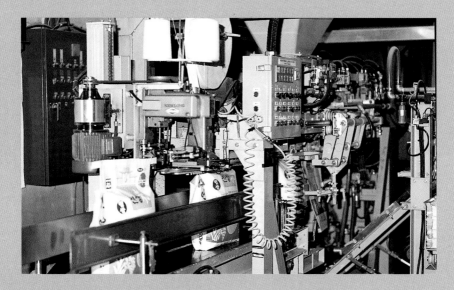

For Transportation

Moving goods and people takes a lot of energy. More than one-fourth of all energy used is for transportation. Some types of transportation, such as cars and buses, are used mainly to move people from one place to another. Trucks, trains, planes, and boats are used not only to move people but also to move goods and freight. Gasoline and diesel fuels are the main types of fuel used in transportation. Planes use a special type of fuel called jet fuel.

Save Energy, Save Earth

Conserving energy now will help make sure that a clean Earth is here for you, your relatives, and your children to enjoy. How can you help? Heating and cooling a house uses 40 percent of the total energy used in a house. To save energy, you can dress in warmer clothing during the winter instead of turning up the heat. You can dress in lighter clothing during warmer weather instead of turning on the air conditioner. Turn the lights off in rooms that are not being used. Switch to compact fluorescent lightbulbs to reduce the energy used. The smallest action, such as taking shorter showers, will help reduce the amount of energy you use. You can make a difference.

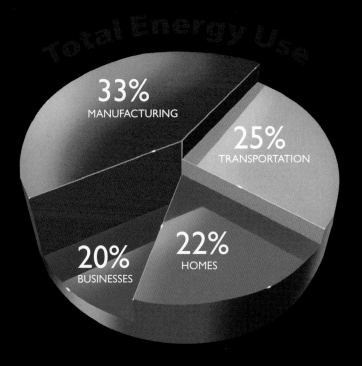

Total Energy Use

33% MANUFACTURING

25% TRANSPORTATION

22% HOMES

20% BUSINESSES

The Future of Energy

All types of energy have one thing in common: They need an energy source. Most of our energy sources today are nonrenewable—once they are used up, they are gone. Coal, nuclear fuel, gas, and other fuels take longer to create than they do to use up. One day they will be gone.

Renewable energy sources, such as the sun, wind, and waves, are naturally replenished in a short time. These energy sources are becoming more and more important as our nonrenewable sources dwindle. Using more renewable energy will allow us to keep up our way of life and protect the supply of Earth's natural resources.

In the future, we will probably need more energy than we are using now. As the world's population grows and uses more technology, more energy will be needed. We will need energy to support the world's technological advances, to explore farther into outer space, and to study the deepest ocean floors. Energy will help us find new medicines, new ways to travel, and new ways to live.

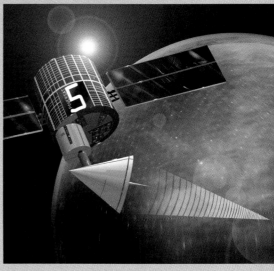

▲ In the future, we may get solar energy delivered from satellites in orbit.

As our world advances, we must continually find new sources of energy and utilize renewable energy sources. In this way, we can power the world of the future and preserve our planet.

Hydrogen Power

Hydrogen power could be the energy of the future. Most people think of hydrogen as one of the atoms in water. Or you might think of the hydrogen bomb that was first used in 1952. But hydrogen may become the fuel of the future.

An engine powered by hydrogen fuel emits less air pollution and makes less noise than traditional car engines. Hydrogen combines with oxygen to make electrical energy. The hydrogen and oxygen produce water as a byproduct. Water vapor is released into the engine's exhaust, an emission that is harmless to the atmosphere. The engine can also run much longer than gasoline or diesel engines before more fuel is needed.

Solar Oven

Energy is power, and it comes in many forms. With a few materials, you can use one of the greatest power sources in the universe—the sun. Sunlight is solar energy. When it is absorbed, it can be used to heat things. In this activity you will be making a solar oven and cooking food with energy from the sun.

Materials

- cardboard box
- aluminum foil
- graham crackers
- chocolate bar
- marshmallows
- sunlight (solar energy)

Procedure

1   Cut the four side corners of the box nearly to the bottom. Pull open slightly.

2   Cover the inside of the box with the aluminum foil. Every side, including the inside of the top, should be covered. The shiny side of the foil should face out. This is a solar oven.

3   Make a s'more by layering marshmallows and pieces of chocolate between two graham crackers.

4 Put the s'more inside the solar oven. Be sure to close the lid of the oven.

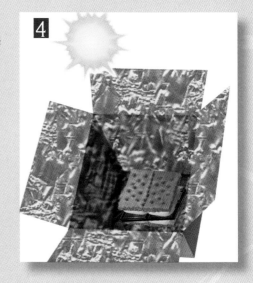

5 Place the solar oven in direct sunlight.

6 Check the s'more every 15 minutes. How long does it take for the s'more to cook? (The chocolate and marshmallow should melt.) What do you observe at each interval?

7 What does the cooked s'more tell you about solar energy? How did energy make the food melt? Try the experiment again with other foods such as bread and butter or bread and cheese. How do they behave differently from the chocolate and marshmallows? How are they the same? What do you think makes the differences?

biomass energy—energy made by burning plant, human, or animal waste

chain reaction—chemical or nuclear reaction in which the reaction keeps itself going

chemical energy—energy locked up in the bonds between atoms and molecules in matter

electrical energy—energy made available by an electrical charge

energy—ability or power to make something move or happen

fission—splitting of atomic nuclei

force—push or pull that can change the state of motion of an object

formula—way to describe how various things relate

fossil fuels—organic fuels made over millions of years that come from the remains of prehistoric animals and plants

generator—machine that produces something, especially electricity

geothermal energy—energy released from heat inside Earth

gravitational energy—energy a body has as a result of being in a gravity field, such as a ball rolling down a hill

hydroelectric power—of or relating to production of electricity by water

kinetic energy—energy of motion

nonrenewable—cannot be replaced

nuclear energy—energy released by splitting the nuclei of atoms in a nuclear power plant

potential energy—energy that is stored

radioactive element—element whose atomic nuclei readily break apart, releasing energy in the form of particles and rays

renewable—can be replaced

solar power—energy from the sun

sound energy—energy in a sound wave

thermal energy—heat energy, caused by the movement of atoms and molecules in matter

turbine—machine with propellers that spin by the pressure of water, steam, or air, and create energy

uranium—radioactive metallic element used in nuclear power stations

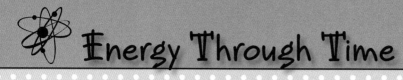

1130	Windmills are first used in Europe
1492	Christopher Columbus notices that a magnetic compass points in different directions at different longitudes
1668	John Wallis suggests the law of conservation of momentum (eventually Newton's third law)
1687	Isaac Newton establishes his three laws of motion and theory of gravity
1752	Benjamin Franklin ties a key to a kite string during a thunderstorm and proves that static electricity and lightning are the same thing
1800s	Coal becomes the principal fuel used by steam-powered trains; more and more households use coal for fuel; coal is used to produce oil and gas to be used for lighting
1800	Alessandro Volta of Italy invents a method for storing electricity in cells, or batteries
1807	Thomas Young uses the term energy in the modern sense of the word
1816	Natural gas is used in Baltimore, Maryland, to fuel street lamps
1860	Wood is primary fuel for heating and cooking in homes and businesses; wood used for steam in industries, trains, and boats
1876	Joseph Swan invents the first incandescent lightbulb
1879	Thomas Edison invents an incandescent lightbulb that can be used for 40 hours without burning out
1881	The Niagara Falls hydropower station opens
1890	Coal displaces much of the wood used in steam generation

1893	A 22-mile (35-km) power line sends electricity from Folsom Powerhouse in California to Sacramento
1900	Ethanol competes with gasoline to be the fuel for cars
1905	Albert Einstein develops his general theory of relativity
1913	A. Goss invents the electric refrigerator
1934	Irène Joliot-Curie and Frédéric Joliot discover artificial radioactivity by bombarding aluminum with alpha particles to obtain radioactive phosphorus
1936	Boulder (later renamed Hoover) Dam in Nevada is completed; a 287-kilovolt power line stretches 266 miles (428 km) from the dam to Los Angeles, California
1945	First nuclear explosion at Alamogordo, New Mexico
1954	The world's first nuclear power plant, in Russia, starts generating electricity; the Atomic Energy Act is passed, allowing private ownership of nuclear reactors; Daryl Chapin, Calvin Fuller, and Gerald Pearson of Bell Labs invent the first solar cell
1957	The Shippingport Reactor in Pennsylvania is the first nuclear power plant to provide electricity to people in the United States
1961	Coal becomes the major fuel used by electric companies in the United States to generate electricity
1973	OPEC oil embargo focuses attention on the energy crisis and results in an increase in demand for U.S. coal

1979	Three Mile Island, Pennsylvania, is the site of the first major nuclear power plant accident
1980	The first commercial geothermal plant in the United States begins operating in Southern California's Imperial Valley
1986	The Clean Coal Technology Act is passed
1989	Siemens A.G. of Munich, West Germany, acquires California-based ARCO Solar, the world's largest solar energy company
1992	The Puna Field in Hawaii begins electrical generation at its geothermal plant
1995	The U.S. Department of Energy identifies nearly 9,000 thermal wells and springs with a geothermal resource greater than 122 degrees F (50 degrees C)
1995	A food-dehydration facility in Empire, Nevada, processes 7,500 tons (6,800 metric tons) of dried onions and garlic per year using geothermal resources
2005	U.S. Congress passes the Energy Policy Act, promoting the use of coal through clean coal technologies
2005	A record-setting hurricane season causes massive damage to the U.S. natural gas and petroleum infrastructure; significant damage is caused along the Gulf of Mexico, where wells, terminals, processing plants, and pipelines are affected; in September, U.S. prices for residential natural gas reach the highest ever recorded
2008	Crude oil prices reach a record high in June 2008—doubling the price from the year before

Albert Einstein (1879–1955)
German physicist best known for his theory of relativity and, specifically, mass-energy equivalence ($E=mc^2$)

Benjamin Franklin (1706–1790)
American politician, inventor, and scientist who proved that lightning is electricity by flying a kite in a storm and extracting electric sparks

Otto Hahn (1879–1968)
German chemist considered to be the pioneer of radioactivity and nuclear chemistry; called the founder of the atomic age

James Maxwell (1831–1879)
Scottish mathematician and physicist who showed that electric and magnetic fields travel through space in the form of waves, at the speed of light

Isaac Newton (1643–1727)
English physicist who described gravity and three laws of motion that came to be called Newton's laws

Alessandro Volta (1745–1827)
Physicist known for the development in 1800 of the first electric cell, a way to store electricity; two or more cells make up a battery

Brallier, Jess M. *Who Was Albert Einstein?* New York: Grosset & Dunlap, 2002.

Fortey, Jacqueline. *Great Scientists.* London: DK, 2007.

Pflaum, Rosalynd. *Marie Curie and Her Daughter Irene.* Minneapolis: Lerner Publications, 1993.

Rosinsky, Natalie M. *Sir Isaac Newton: Brilliant Mathematician and Scientist.* Minneapolis: Compass Point Books, 2008.

Tracy, Kathleen. *Pierre and Marie Curie and the Discovery of Radium.* Hockessin, Del.: Mitchell Lane Publishers, 2005.

Whiting, Jim. *John Dalton and the Atomic Theory.* Hockessin, Del.: Mitchell Lane Publishers, 2005.

On the Web

For more information on this topic, use FactHound.

1. Go to *www.facthound.com*
2. Choose your grade level.
3. Begin your search.

This book's ID number is 9780756539672

FactHound will find the best sites for you.

Index

Don Herweck

Don Herweck was born and educated in Southern California and has degrees in math, physics, and physical science. Currently he is an operations manager for a large automotive manufacturer and travels internationally and throughout the United States for his business. He is the father of four children and has recently returned to California after several years living in the South and Midwest.

Image Credits

Energy /